# Positive Power of
# Thanksgiving

## J. P. VASWANI

Compiled By: Dr. (Mrs.) Prabha Sampath
Krishna Kumari

**A Sterling Paperback**

STERLING PAPERBACKS
An imprint of
Sterling Publishers (P) Ltd.
A-59, Okhla Industrial Area, Phase-II,
New Delhi-110020.
Tel: 26387070, 26386209; Fax: 91-11-26383788
E-mail: info@sterlingpublishers.com
www.sterlingpublishers.com

*Positive Power of Thanksgiving*
© 2005, J.P. Vaswani
ISBN 81 207 2899 8

*Published by* Sterling Publishers Pvt. Ltd., New Delhi-110020.
*Printed at* Sterling Publishers Pvt. Ltd., New Delhi-110020.

# Contents

# Foreword

In an era when this world of ours is ruthlessly attacked by the tumultous waves of violence and injustice, when poverty, both material and spiritual, reigns supreme in many corners of the globe, when disharmony seems to be the order of the day, it is not unusual, at times, to feel helplessly adrift in a sea of doubt, anxiety and uncertainty.

What can possibly come to our rescue? It is nothing other than our gratitude – gratitude to God. If anything on earth can sustain our golden connecting link with God, our Source, then that very thing is gratitude, sincere gratitude – our sincere gratitude to our inner Pilot. Gratitude performs miracles. Gratitude expands our receptivity to God's Light. Gratitude strengthens our physical body, purifies our vital energy, widens our mental vision and intensifies our inner happiness.

How to cultivate gratitude in the very depths of our hearts? From the compassionate heart and illumined mind of the path-finding seer-philosopher Dada J.P. Vaswani, comes *Positive Power of Thanksgiving*, through which he provides a failsafe approach to the fountain-art of gratitude.

Within these pages shines Dadaji's God-given boon as a communicator *non-pareil*. Employing an ingenious amalgam of humorous anecdotes and thought-provoking parables, sublime sentiments and practical techniques, Dadaji most effectively captivates the readers, as he instructs and entertains, coaxes and cajoles and moves us to experience the ever-deepening gratitude-heart, liberating us from the fetters of depression, frustration and hopelessness so that we can run the fastest to our destined goal.

Dadaji's wisdom-flooded advice runs thus:

> ...*the positive gifts that thankfulness confers upon us are very many. It fills your life with peace, joy and serenity. It banishes negative thinking – for gratitude and complaints, gratitude and worry, gratitude and anxiety just cannot exist together!*

Dadaji soulfully adds that, no matter the condition or circumstance of life:

*...When we thank the Lord all the time, we build for ourselves a ladder of consciousness on which we can climb and touch the very pinnacle of peace.*

Gratitude must not only be felt, but revealed – expressed in word and in action. And this expression of gratitude must be extended to God and our fellow human beings alike. Through a series of well-crafted narratives, Dadaji shows us how the exchange of gratitude and appreciation can have a mutually uplifting and life-transforming effect on both giver and receiver.

Dadaji's lofty vision of the inner world and, at the same time, his most brilliant outer arguments, are rooted in spirituality, science, practicality and commonsense:

*When you thank God or thank a fellow human being, your heart expands. This strengthens the immune system...Recent medical research indicates that positive emotions like love and gratitude actually enhance the immune system, which is the body's shield against attack from disease and illness.*

Following in the hallowed footsteps of his beloved Master, Sadhu Vaswani, on the strength of his sleepless love and self-offering for the betterment of all living beings, Dadaji most effectively conveys his world-transformation messages.

*Positive Power of Thanksgiving* embodies and reveals the secret of secrets to a life of true fulfilment. Dadaji's clarion call to the heart of mankind:

> *Let go of your problems. Let God take over! Live like a child. Surrender yourself to the Lord in this childlike trust and you will find miracles happening in your daily life…let go, let go, let God!…Letting go permits divine ideas to flow, divine light to shine, divine power to work, divine order and righteousness to bless your life.*

A consummate book of our times, *Positive Power of Thanksgiving* is destined to be universally loved and treasured by seekers of all faiths, for generations to come, and for this extremely rich and unreserved contribution, we all owe the divinely loved and supremely adored Master Dadaji an unending debt of gratitude.

*Sri Chinmoy*

✱  ✱

We are profoundly grateful to Sri Chinmoy of the UN Peace Meditation Foundation for having kindly contributed this wonderful Foreward. A prolific writer and a gifted composer, Sri Chinmoy has been closely associated with the UN since the 1970's. Sri Chinmoy had, conferred on Revered Dada, J. P. Vaswani the prestigious U Thant Peace Award in April, 1998.

# Two Magic Words

Thank you!

I regard these two words to be the two most important words in the English language.

Which of us would not like to hear these two words addressed to us? Parents appreciate it when children come to say "Thank you", to them. Children are thrilled when parents say "Thank you"! Teachers feel fulfilled when students utter these magic words. Why, even God feels happy when you thank Him for His many favours and blessings so munificently conferred upon you!

Would you agree that even God appreciates it when you thank Him for His mercy? So let me tell you a story about Jesus.

Once, Jesus was on his way to Jerusalem. On the long, narrow, dusty road between Samaria and Galilee, he came across a row of lepers, who were standing at some distance from the road, huddled together in a group.

In those days leprosy was regarded as a deadly, infectious disease. Lepers were not allowed to mix with the people. In fact, they were not even allowed to present themselves before the eyes of their 'clean' and 'healthy' brothers. They were condemned to live in caves and catacombs outside human settlements. Food and clothes in the form of pitiful alms were dumped near their site, so that they would not venture out to seek food or other forms of relief.

When the group of lepers saw Jesus approaching, they cried out in desperation and misery, "Master! heal us! For only you can help us in our affliction. We pray Master, heal us!"

Jesus looked at them with compassion. Nine of them were Jews, and one of them was a Samaritan. In those days, the Jews regarded themselves as superior, while the Samaritans were treated as outcastes. However, the common bond of suffering and affliction had united these men together in a brotherhood of despair. Together, they cried out again and again, "Master! Heal us!"

Jesus looked at them with loving compassion and said to them, "Go to the priest!"

Now, the lepers were puzzled. They had put all their faith in Jesus. Why did he want them to go to the priest? However, the Master had spoken, and they obeyed him implicitly. They turned to walk in the direction of the Temple.

Hardly had they walked a few halting paces, when they became aware of a strange sensation. They felt their spirits lifting, their hearts became light, vigour returned to their limbs, at the same time, the hideous sores on their body began to disappear and melt away, and their very skin became smooth as that of a new born baby. They saw one another's faces becoming radiant and beautiful! It was a miracle!

"We are healed!" they exclaimed, jubiliant and elated. "We are healed! We are healed!"

Amidst their ecstasy and self-congratulations, they remembered their families who had been bereft with grief. "Let us rush to our loved ones," they said to one another. "Let us give them the good news that we are now healed and whole again! Let us share this wonderful moment with our near and dear ones!"

In a moment, the nine Jews had rushed off in the direction of their homes. But the Samaritan lingered.

"Yes," he mused, "I must go back to my family...but before I do, I must return to the Master and thank Him for the miraculous gift that He has bestowed upon me!"

The Samaritan rushed to catch up with Jesus. He fell at Jesus's feet and said to the Lord with tears in his eyes, "Master! My gratitude to you. You have healed me and given me a new lease of life! Thank you, thank you, thank you!"

Jesus blessed the Samaritan and said: "Ten were cleansed, but only one has come. Where are the other nine?"

Even God misses something when you don't express your gratitude!

In everything, give thanks.

*Thessalonians 5:18*

Gratitude is the heart's memory.

*French proverb*

# Why Should You Thank God?

People often choose very selfish and narrow reasons to thank God. Businessmen offer thanks when they make a fat profit. Students offer thanks when they pass examinations. In India, elaborate thanks are offered to God when a son is born!

However, a true seeker learns to give thanks to God for very different reasons. He knows that this human birth itself is the greatest of gifts that God has bestowed on him – for it is the means, the instrument by which he can seek his salvation. He knows that birth into this world is the necessary prerequisite to gain ultimate freedom from the cycle of birth–death–rebirth.

And God has made this world of ours a beautiful place to be born into! It is not as if we have to endure living here under harsh and trying conditions, until death relieves us of the burden of existence.

Look around you for a moment. Marvel at the vastness of the blue sky the splendour of the sun, moon and stars that appear and set without fail, the soft and gentle touch of the breeze against your face, the loveliness of the landscape, the majesty of the mountains, the mystery of the deep forests, the serenity of the lake, the steady flow of the river, the rise and fall of the tides in the dark, deep, blue ocean – is it not all beautiful, sublime and elevating?

Consider too, the marvellous mechanism that is the human body. Shakespeare's Hamlet exclaims:

> What a piece of work is man! How noble in reason! How infinite in faculty! In form and moving, how express and admirable! In action, how like an angel! In apprehension, how like a god! The beauty of the world, the paragon of animals...

Can the most sophisticated digital camera equal the human eye? Can the most expensive audio equipment match the human ear? Can man ever devise a motor that can replicate the human heart? And what super computer can match the human brain in agility, memory, association and recognition?

Count your blessings and thank God every living, waking, moment – for God's generosity to you is infinite!

# Not me, but Him!

Human beings are much given to self-congratulations on the least pretext. Every little success or achievement is enough to boost our ego. "I have accomplished that!" "I succeeded in doing this!" we boast, all too often.

A very interesting story is related in the *Mahabharata*. The Kurukshetra war was over, and Sri Krishna had departed the earth. Arjuna was travelling across a strange country when he was attacked by robbers.

Now Arjuna was a fearless warrior, and had been the leading light of the Pandava forces in winning the war. Further, his weapons were all divine gifts. Therefore, he fought valiantly against his attackers – but it was to no avail. He was beaten and robbed.

Miserable and despondent, he sought out Sage Ved Vyas and begged him to explain the inexplicable – how was it that he, the invincible Arjuna with his incomparable valour and weapons, faced defeat at the hands of a few ruffians?

Ved Vyas explained to him that neither he, nor his weapons, had possessed any intrinsic power. "Your invincibility came from the presence of the Lord who was your Divine Charioteer. It was His power that infused your weapons with their might. Now that He is no longer with you, these weapons are useless. You fight now on your own feeble strength."

Arjuna's eyes were opened to a great truth. Man achieves all that he does only through the sanction and grace of the Divine Will!

We are only too apt to regard our cleverness, our skill, our diplomacy, our tact, and our efficiency as the sole reason for our success. A little reflection will make us realise that it is the Divine Presence that guides us at every step. Therefore, success and accomplishment should teach us humility instead of ·pride, and prompt us to express our gratitude to God.

Every accomplishment, every form of excellence, every success, small or big, belongs to God. If you are wise and intelligent, it is God-given. If your hard work and effort are commendable, it is due to the grace of God. If you are truly conscious of this and acknowledge His grace in all humility – why, this humility too is a manifestation of His mercy upon you!

When you learn to thank the Lord in prosperity and plenty, you will also grow in the realisation that you owe thanks to Him in adversity and misery as well. For every disappointment in your life is His appointment. He upsets your plans, only to set up His own! When you learn to thank the Lord in all conditions, you will grow in the realisation that you are but an instrument of His Divine Will – and is that not a wonderful thing to be grateful for?

In prayer, let us ask for less, Thank more!

Thank the Lord for His mercies which endure from everlasting to everlasting!

*– J.P. Vaswani*

Thanksgiving is a sure index of spiritual health.

*Maurice Dametz*

# Thanksgiving Is Here And Now!

Offering thanks to God teaches us one of the most valuable lessons of life – to appreciate the here and now. We learn to stop wishing for what-might-have-been and yearning for what-is-not, and enjoy what *is, now.* So we offer thanks, we focus on the present moment and experience the full wonder of the precious present moment.

A friend of mine who worked in a company at Pune, was transferred to Mumbai. He was so upset, that whenever I met him, he had nothing but complaints about the city. "I hate the noise and the pollution," he groaned. "This is just a concrete jungle," he would say. "The traffic is terrible!" and "I can't stand the mad rush of this city!"

I lost touch with him for a few years, until he came to see me in Pune. I asked him how he was doing in Mumbai, and was surprised to learn that he was back in Pune now.

"That must make you happy!" I remarked.

"Do you know, I miss Mumbai!" he said. "Whatever anyone says, it is a vibrant city – a city full of life! It spoils you, it changes you! If you have been happy in Mumbai, you just can't be happy anywhere else! I find Pune dull and boring after Mumbai."

How easy it is for us to overlook those gifts we have when we focus on those that we lack! We only diminish the value of what we are and where we are, if we do not pause to be thankful for the present.

Here are a few suggestions to help you appreciate the here and the now:

- Imagine what your condition would be if you lost all that you have now.
- Each day, make a list of all the things – big and small – for which you are grateful. Stay conscious of them throughout the day.
- Help those who are less fortunate than you are and feel grateful to God for having given you an opportunity of being a blessing to some in need. This will surely give you a new perspective to life.

I often urge my friends to count their blessings. However, many of them tell me there are very few to count!

Many of us try to count our blessings on our fingers – and find that they are not too many. However, the wise ones are aware that the blessings we have received from Him are infinite. Every moment of the day, every aspect of your mind, intellect, body – all these are God's gifts to you.

## Thanksgiving Is Perpetual

In America, they celebrate the fourth Thursday in November as Thanksgiving Day every year. It is indeed a wonderful tradition.

The roots of this beautiful custom date back to 1621, when the Pilgrim Fathers, as they were called, first arrived in America after a long and arduous journey across the Atlantic. Here, after a difficult winter in which they lost several of their loved ones, a winter also marked by great starvation and privation, they reaped a rich harvest in the new land, and offered Thanksgiving to the Lord with a special service. After successive federal proclamations, the whole of America observes Thanksgiving Day as a national holiday. It is marked by church services, family reunions and sumptuous dinners.

However, there are many Americans who rue the fact that like many other national and religious holidays, Thanksgiving has also become highly commercialised. People have forgotten what they are supposed to be giving thanks for. In fact, in a recently conducted survey, people on the street were asked, "What stands out in your mind when you think of Thanksgiving Day?" The answers received were: Turkey Dinner, Fall, Pumpkins, Corn, etc.

My American friends often ask me, "Why is it that Indians don't observe a Thanksgiving Day?"

My answer to them is, "Every day in India is a Thanksgiving Day – for we have to thank God for all that we are and all that we have, every day of our lives!"

We cannot, indeed, confine our Thanksgiving to any single day. Ideally every day, every moment of every day should be an occasion of Thanksgiving. The spirit of Thanksgiving should so infuse our life that it should transform our life into a constant remembrance of His infinite mercy to us!

Have you heard of the man who wished to dispose of his home? He went to his friend in the real estate business and asked him to help him sell the house, after describing the house and garden to him as well as he could. The friend wrote out an advertisement on the basis of what he had heard, and read it out to the owner.

"Beautiful 50's house set in spacious garden," he read. "Gabled roof, spacious verandas, well-ventilated rooms and large dining/drawing rooms. Ideally suited for families with children."

"Read that again," said the owner. His friend obliged.

"This house is not for sale," said the man. "All my life I've wanted a place like the one you have just described. But I never knew I had it until I heard what you have written."

It requires wisdom and perception to appreciate the here and now.

## How May I Thank Him?

Normally, the act of saying "Thank You" puts a certain distance between the giver and the receiver. Some people even say "Thanks" automatically, without so much as looking up at the person they are giving thanks to, or even meeting his/her eyes.

My friends tell me this is how one buys a newspaper in England:

You: Can I have *The Times* please?

Shopkeeper: Certainly, here it is.

You: Thank you. How much is it?

Shopkeeper: Fifty pence please.

You: Here is a pound. Thank you.

Shopkeeper: Thank you! Here is your change.

You: Thank you – and good-bye!

How very polite and courteous! But many people pay merely lip service with their "Thanks"; the word loses its meaning when it is uttered mechanically.

God should not be thanked in such a superficial, mechanical way.

The dynamic way of Thanksgiving is to make your life an offering to the Lord. Affirm to Him that you are His, and that all your words, deeds and thoughts are dedicated to His glory.

Here is a little prayer that I often say:

O Lord, I seek neither wealth, nor power, nor the pleasures of this or the next world.

25

I need Thee and Thee alone!

Grant me the gift of longing – deep yearning – for Thy Lotus Feet!

Grant me the gift of tears – that I may keep awake at night and meditate and, during the daytime, help as many as I can, to lift the load on the rough road of life!

I thank Thee Lord, for Thy infinite mercy on me!

Who does not thank for little, will not thank for much.

*Estonian proverb*

A thankful heart is not only the greatest virtue, but the parent of all other virtues.

*Cicero*

# Are You Truly Thankful?

When someone gives you a gift, they like to see you using it, enjoying it and appreciating their thoughtfulness in choosing it for you. This makes them truly happy, for they feel that their gift is well bestowed, well utilised.

If someone gives you a book, they ask, "Have you read it? Did you like it?"

If you leave the book on the shelf, unread, you do not utilise the gift. It is devalued – and therefore, your thanks loses much of its meaning.

So it is with God's gifts. It is only when you utilise them in the best possible way, that your Thanksgiving is true and sincere.

The Vedic prayer goes thus:

*Sarve bhavantu sukinah:*
*Sarve santu niraamayaah:*
*Sarve bhadraani pashyantu:*
*Ma kaschit dukha bhagbhavet.*

May all be happy. May everyone enjoy good health. May everyone see what is auspicious. May everyone be free from the misery of diseases and suffering!

What a beautiful attitude this prayer teaches us! If only each one of us holds this attitude in our hearts, and sends out vibrations of good-will and love to all around us, we are expressing the best form of thanks to God!

## Cultivate the Spirit of Thankfulness

The Roman philosopher Cicero said: "Gratitude is not only the greatest of virtues, but the parent of all the others."

A heart filled with gratitude is one that promotes joyous living. And the positive gifts that thankfulness confers upon us are many. It fills your life with peace, joy and serenity. It banishes negative thinking – for gratitude and complaints, gratitude and worry, gratitude and anxiety just cannot exist together!

Thankfulness makes you young in spirit – for it enables you to behold the miraculous hand of God in everything you see around you. Children are blessed with this great gift – and their enthusiasm and exuberance are quite infectious. However, as we grow older, we lose this sense of joy and begin to take things for granted. We become jaded and cynical. Let us thank God again and again, if we wish to keep the child in us alive!

Thankfulness makes us nice people to be with – we will find people drawn to us; we will see that we make more and more friends.

People who are prone to complaints and self-pity are seldom liked. They are shunned by their friends and colleagues, for they only pass on their crankiness and dullness to others. On the other hand, cheerful, spirited people exude confidence and optimism. The mood around them is upbeat and positive. They not only make new friends easily – they retain all their old friends too, which is no easy feat in this age of passing relationships and nodding acquaintances.

Thankfulness is the perfect antidote to negative emotions like depression, frustration, resentment and bitterness. When we fail to appreciate our gifts and our friends, our spiritual evolution is thwarted and our minds are darkened. Gratitude is the light that can illumine us inside and brighten the environment we live in.

Gratitude also helps us grow in the spirit of tolerance and acceptance. The world we live in is far from perfect; we are not ourselves paragons of perfection; and the same goes for the people around us. As they say, it's a crazy, mixed-up world, but we must recognise ourselves as part of all this imperfection and accept life as it comes.

Thankfulness leads us on to generous giving and sharing. The more grateful you are, the more you are inclined to share what you have with others. In this, as in so much else, the more we give, the more we get – whether it is gifts, wealth, love or friendship.

Thankfulness banishes worry and anxiety. Where there is constant worry, there is no room for happiness. And worrying is a compulsive habit. We worry about money; we worry about our health; we worry about our loved ones. Most of our worries relate to a distant, unknown future. On the other hand, thankfulness helps us to focus on the present – the appreciation of the here and the now. Gratitude focuses us on the present moment and we realise that tomorrow is another day!

Here are a few lines I read from Melody Beattie:

Gratitude unlocks the fullness of life. It turns what we have into enough and more. It turns denial into acceptance, chaos into order, and confusion to clarity. Gratitude makes sense of our past, brings peace for today and creates a vision for tomorrow.

One of life's gifts is that each of us, no matter how tired and downtrodden, finds reasons for thankfulness.

*—J. Robert Maskin*

Some people are always grumbling because roses have thorns; I am thankful that thorns have roses.

*—Alphonse Karr*

# The Therapy Of Thanksgiving

Whenever, I speak to people of the Therapy of Thanksgiving, they invariably turn round and ask me, "What is this therapy you speak of? What therapeutic value can thanksgiving have? We don't really see what connection health can have with thanksgiving!"

My answer is simple! When you thank God or thank a fellow human being, your heart expands. This strengthens the immune system.

Recent medical research indicates that positive emotions like love and gratitude actually enhance the immune system, which is the body's shield against attack from disease and illness. Our mental attitude and our psychological condition have a direct bearing on the immune system. Positive feelings of gratitude and joy release endorphines into the blood stream, which are the body's natural painkillers. They are said to stimulate dilation of the blood vessels and relaxation of the cardiac muscles, thus strengthening the body's capacity to resist disease and promote recovery.

On the other hand negative emotions such as anger, grief and bitterness are known to dump high levels of adrenaline in the blood. This constricts blood vessels, raises blood pressure and increases stress upon the heart. It also slows down the movement of white blood cells which fight disease and enhances our immunity.

In other words, gratitude releases happy hormones and inhibits the 'unhappy' hormones in our system thus helping us to live longer and healthier lives. If you are too sceptical to believe this, let me tell you, gratitude may not cure you of cancer, but it will definitely make you feel better!

There is a story about the famous actress and singer, Ethel Walters. Once she was flying to Atlanta, when a commotion arose in the plane, which was about to take off in a few minutes. A middle-aged man had come on board, excessively drunk. He was demanding one more drink, and the stewardess had a problem finding him a seat, for his fellow passengers objected to his condition.

Reluctantly, the stewardess asked Miss Walters if she could seat the man next to her.

"Let him sit down beside me," Ethel Walters said graciously. "I shall watch over him."

The man slipped into his seat and immediately asked for a drink.

"Why don't you have some food, my friend?" she said to him.

"I can't eat a thing," he wailed. "I only want another drink."

She saw that he was a deeply troubled man. "I don't know what's making you so miserable, my friend," she said gently. "Whatever it is, you can't drown it with drink. It's just not the right way to handle your problems. There's always help available for you when you need it," she added.

He poured his heart out to her then and there. He had a beautiful and talented daughter. She had invited him to a concert where she was going to sing. But he had not been able to make it. Now, tragically, she was dead, killed in an automobile accident – and he was flying out to Atlanta to attend her funeral! No wonder he was miserable. He simply could not forgive himself.

34

"There's no need to feel like that," Ethel Walters told him. "I know there's someone who loves you and He will surely help you!"

She coaxed him to eat a little food and then go to sleep. He fell asleep with his head on her shoulder.

Ethel Waters was, at that time, no longer in her prime; she was old and rheumatic. Her shoulder and arm became numb as the man's head rested on her – but she did not move a muscle. She only prayed, "Thank you Lord, for looking after this poor man. Thank you, Lord, for letting him sleep a while."

When they reached Atlanta, she asked the stewardess for a wet towel and woke her friend up. He wiped his face and got ready to leave. He was now completely sober. "I don't know how to thank you," he said to the singer.

"Thank the Lord, my friend," she said to him. "You may have slept on my shoulder during this flight, but remember, you always have God's shoulder to lean on. He will always be there to love you and take care of you."

Whenever you happen to feel tired, dispirited, discouraged and unable to cope, just thank the Lord for being there with you. You will find that your unhappy, negative thoughts drain away, and the energy of God flows into you, to make you positive and whole!

President Dwight D. Eisenhower led America during troubled times. Whenever he was overwhelmed by problems and difficulties, he turned to the Lord at the end of the day. "Thank you, God for helping me throughout this day," he would say. "Whenever I thought about you, you helped me make good decisions. Whenever I forgot you and depended on my own limited intelligence, I didn't do so well! I have had a tough day, Lord, and I am tired. I am going to sleep now, and I beg you to take over and run the country for me while I am asleep. Thank you for everything!"

With that, he would peacefully drop off to sleep!

Have you ever learnt the art and science of *reiki* which heals by the therapy of touch? The first thing that a *reiki* practitioner does when he starts to give *reiki* is to reinforce what is called "the attitude of gratitude." It is this that is the basis of *reiki* healing – the therapy of thankfulness that allows all that is positive and wholesome in the Universe to flow into you!

There was a man who suffered a severe nervous breakdown. He became so depressed and debilitated that he became like a ghost of his former self – for he had been a dynamic, vital, energetic man in the past. His doctors could do nothing to make him feel better. Finally, a friend suggested that he should try the therapy of thanksgiving.

"Therapy of thanksgiving? What's that?" the man wanted to know.

"Make a list of all the people who have helped you in your life," the friend advised him. "Send out thoughts of gratitude to as many of them as you can remember.

"Better still, choose someone, anyone you like, and actually write a letter of thanks, expressing your appreciation for his or her help to you."

The first person who came to the man's mind was his school teacher, who, years ago, had instilled in him an appreciation for poetry. On an impulse he picked up a pen and paper and wrote the lady a thank you note, telling her how much her efforts had meant to him.

The teacher was by then an old lady, long retired. But she wrote back to say how thrilled she was with his letter. "Your's is the first letter of thanks I have ever received from any of my students," she wrote. "I shall always cherish your letter."

Beginning to feel better, the man started writing thank you notes to one person after another, until he had written more than 500 such letters! Sure enough, he was back to normal, back at his work. Later, whenever he tended to feel depressed, he would do the same, and let the therapy of thanksgiving work for him.

How does thanksgiving heal and strengthen you? When you focus on the attitude of gratitude, you focus on all that is good and positive in your life. As all that is good and positive emanates from God, the person who practises the therapy of thanksgiving allows the most positive and powerful forces in the world to flow into him, and draws strength and healing therefrom. It is infact, akin to being connected with a powerful spiritual dynamo!

A friend of mine lost an eye in an accident. He was taken to the hospital.

Several friends visited him in the hospital to sympathise with him in his great and irreparable loss.

They were surprised to find him as cheerful as ever.

When they mentioned this to him, he replied, "I thank God that one of my eyes still remains. I can learn to use it well, and I am confident that I can see with it well, and I am confident that I can see with it all that I saw when I had two eyes. The accident could have robbed me of both my eyes, but God chose to protect one of them for me! Thanks be to God! Blessed be His Name!"

The accident, which would have plunged a lesser man into a slough of despondency, did not seem to touch him! He drew inner strength from his therapy of thankfulness!

The expression of gratitude is a rich and positive exercise. It is a mental and spiritual tonic. When you allow your thankfulness to be expressed, you are affirming God's goodness and grace. This always works to your own benefit – for you become hopeful, optimistic and happy.

Dwelling on the attitude of gratitude makes us open and receptive to the Lord's blessings. And we find that good things come to pass in our life.

Have you had a bad day? Thank the Lord it's over – thank Him for helping you cope with it while it lasted. When we do this, defeats are turned into victories, as we imbibe strength from our struggles.

The sign outside the gates of salvation says, "Be grateful."

– *Michael Levine*

Into the well which supplies thee with water, cast no stones.

– *Talmud*

# PRACTICAL SUGGESTIONS

## Practical Suggestion No. 1
## Begin the Day with Thanks to the Lord!

*Utthishta! Jagruta!* Arise! Awake!

Swami Vivekananda used these words from the *Vedas* to galvanise the youth of India into action.

Awakening to a new day is a beautiful experience. Zen masters teach us that waking up is a special process. We must remind ourselves again and again that being alive is a miracle which we may have lost sight of when we were asleep. How exhilarating it is to recognise and reaffirm the miracle by offering thanks to the Lord!

When we awake, we wake to the wonder of being alive. In this recognition, gratitude flows out of us like a clear mountain stream.

William Ward tells us: "God gives you a gift of 86,400 seconds everyday. Use the first one to say *Thank You!*"

To be alive, to be able to see, to be able to hear, walk, talk – aren't all of these great gifts to thank God for? Just to be alive is the greatest blessing, as the deeply spiritual poetess, Emily Dickinson writes: "The mere sense of living is joy enough." We need to assert this joy, this sense of wonder, every morning when we awake.

I always tell my friends: "The past is a cancelled cheque. The future is a promissory note. The present is the only cash in hand. Use it wisely and well."

It is essential that we celebrate the exquisite sense of awareness of the present moment, especially when we wake up. Let not the regrets for the irretrievable past or worries for the unknown future blur the glory of the day that is dawning upon us. Let us begin the day by offering thanks to the Lord.

Life may be tough – but it is also wonderful! Every day we receive afresh the chance to live, love, work and play – and to make better human beings of ourselves. Should we not thank the Lord as we start each day?

Here are a few beautiful lines I read somewhere:

Normal day, let me be aware of the treasure you are.

Let me learn from you, love you, bless you before you depart.

Let me not pass you by in quest of some rare and perfect tomorrow.

Let me hold you while I may, for it may not always be so...

Our journey upon this earth is meant to take us onward, forward, upward, Godward! Out of the very depths of our heart must awaken the cry, "I have need of You, Lord! I cannot live without You."

When we grow in this realisation, we attain the stage of spiritual awakening. When you begin the day with this awareness, something stirs deep within you and your life becomes new, you are filled with light and warmth, joy and peace. You exclaim with the great Russian writer, Leo Tolstoy: "To know God is to live!"

The secret of the new life is love of God. We affirm this love again and again when we begin each and every day with thanks to the Lord.

"How can I keep on saying, Thank you God, day after day?" a young man said to me. "Won't God be tired of listening to those words?"

I asked him, "How many times do you tell your girl friend that you love her?"

"Oh, several times!" was his answer.

"Does she not feel tired of listening to the same words over and over again?" I enquired.

"No way!" he replied firmly. "She is thrilled to hear those words every time I utter them."

"I think you have answered your own question," I said to him.

Another depressing question I am asked is this: *"What is there to be thankful for?"*

I am afraid we are taking our life for granted. How many of us feel, when we wake up in the morning, "It is wonderful to be alive!"

The great American philosopher, Thoreau was an inspired thinker whose life and writings were a great influence on Mahatma Gandhi. Thoreau once observed that every human being ought to give thanks atleast once every day for the fact that he was born. Thoreau said that he himself did this every day.

I am truly distressed when I hear some people moan, "I wish I hadn't been born!" I am sure they don't really mean it.

Are you one of those people who occasionally feels this way? Then let me recommend to you what Norman Vincent Peale calls his 'last-time technique'.

It works like this – when you are doing something wonderful, enjoyable or worthwhile, ask yourself, "Suppose this were the last time I am doing this...?"

How would you feel if you knew that it was the last time you are seeing a beautiful sunset, the last time you are listening to your favourite piece of music, the last time you enjoy being with your loved ones...

It is just a mental trick. But it works! And when you affirm the spirit of thankfulness at the dawn of a new day, rich blessings will flow into your life!

If you wake up in the morning and think, like the people I mentioned earlier, that there is nothing to be thankful for – then you are not being positive. One of the greatest things to be thankful for is the undeniable fact that you are not alone: God is with you!

---

It is a dangerous thing to ask why someone else has been given more. It is humbling – and indeed healthy – to ask why you have been given so much.

*–Condoleezza Rice*

# Practical Suggestion No. 2
## Count Your Blessings!

Once, a man asked me, " Have you ever had a sleepless night?"

I said, I have indeed. There are days when the body is overworked, fatigued and so exhausted that sleep eludes us. I'm sure all of us have gone through this experience at one time or another and I am no exception.

"I'll tell you what you can do to overcome sleeplessness," he said to me enthusiastically. "You must count sheep."

"I think I have a better method, my friend," I replied with a smile. " I count my blessings instead! "

Indeed, I find I have so much to be grateful to God for! The great gift of this human birth; my wonderful parents who brought me into this beautiful world, and sowed seeds of character in my plastic mind; the members of my family, my brothers and sisters; my loving kind friends and above all my beloved Master and Mentor, Sadhu Vaswani, whose grace has been the most inspiring influence on my life.

When I count my blessings, I keep on thanking the Lord. This induces the marvellous and restful feeling that God is in His heaven and all is well with this world.

The Zen Master, Ling Chi said that the real miracle is not to walk on water, in the air, or on burning charcoal, but *just to walk on earth.* How wonderful for us to stop and breathe in the awareness that the world is a beautiful place; that being alive is a vital, joyous experience; and that life is the greatest miracle of all!

It is a sad fact that many people spend most of their lives waiting for disasters to strike. We need to cultivate the belief that the universe is friendly, that life is benevolent, that good things will happen to us and that even if bad things happen, they can make us better and wiser!

Have you ever come upon a field full of flowers? Have you got up to watch the glorious sunrise that happens morning after morning? Have you felt the gentle breeze brush your face and ruffle your hair? Have you inhaled the scented night air and looked at the moon and stars with awe and wonder?

Have you ever stopped to ask yourself at such moments, what have I done to deserve these marvellous gifts?

The answer is that none of us ever did anything to earn these gifts nor do they make demands upon us for return or repayment. They are just there; they are ours for the asking!

In polite circles, it is expected that people say "Thank you" for every little thing others do for their benefit. People thank waiters who serve them in restaurants. The senior executive thanks his secretary who organises his appointments. We thank the telephone operator who gets us the connection we seek. Even the disembodied voices on the answering machines of banks and business enterprises thank us for calling them!

Expressing one's gratitude is considered a mark of politeness, courtesy and good breeding. Is it not fitting then, that we extend such politeness and courtesy to God who has given us so much to be grateful for?

Let not your gratitude stop with words.

Gratitude is appreciation; gratitude is goodwill; gratitude is a benevolent and warm feeling for someone who has helped us, been good to us in one way or another.

But our gratitude must not stop with words alone. It must be expressed through actions or it will remain superficial.

God supplies our every need and always keeps us under His Divine protection. This awareness will help us to feel grateful to God at every step and in every round of life.

To express this spirit of gratitude in the best possible way, we must utilise our God given gifts as best as we can. Our body, mind, senses and intellect are amazing gifts, and we need to put them to the best possible use.

Consider a young man whose father has given him a sophisticated and advanced computer. He thanks his dad, of course. But he uses his computer to play mindless games and nothing more. Is this really the spirit of gratitude?

Let us learn to translate our thanksgiving into action. Let us use our God-given gifts to promote unity, harmony, peace and joy in this world. Only then are we truly thanking our Creator for this marvellous gift of human birth.

Let us give thanks for this beautiful day. Let us give thanks for this life. Let us give thanks for the water without which life would not be possible. Let us give thanks to grandmother Earth who protects and nourishes us.

*— Daily Prayer of the Lakota American Indian*

## Practical Suggestion No.3
## Cultivate a Sense of Wonder

Have you seen a child greet his mother when she returns to him after a short absence? He is so thrilled, his eyes sparkle, he beams and smiles so beautifully.

Watch a little girl being given a cone of ice-cream. Her delight knows no bounds.

Take a little boy to a zoo. Watch his eyes widen in wonder and amazement as he sees the elephant and the giraffe and the zebra. " Can there be anything more remarkable than these creatures?" his expression seems to say.

In this sense of wonder and awe, children leave us far behind. Wonder is the recognition that life is magnificent and glorious. It leads us naturally into an attitude of thankfulness.

Let us allow ourselves to be overwhelmed by the myriad glories of life, the many splendours of human relationships, and the daily miracles that happen around us all the time! Let us not allow our sense of wonder to become jaded and numb.

When the well-known preacher and writer of inspirational books, Norman Vincent Peale, was a young man, he had a very difficult time coping with a few tough problems that had cropped up in his life. He took his problems to an older, trusted friend, to whom he complained, "Why can't I cope with these problems?"

The friend reflected for a while and then suggested, "Maybe it's because you are not grateful enough."

Peale was perplexed. What did he mean by 'not grateful enough'?

The older man explained about what he held to be the law of life: focus on your troubles and they will multiply; count your blessings, and your life will grow more and more joyous.

"My advice to you Norman," he concluded, "is that you become less of a complainer and more of a thanks-giver. I assure you that you will be able to manage all your problems."

Peale found that this advice really worked. "In some unfathomable way," he writes, "the acknowledgement of past blessings seems to be the activation of new blessings."

> When eating bamboo sprouts, remember the man who planted them.
>
> — *Chinese proverb*
>
> Again and again, O Lord! has Thy mercy shone upon me in my pilgrimage.
>
> The mercy I hold in my memory in gratitude and love.
>
> Let me hold it everyday in my life!
>
> — *Sadhu Vaswani*

## Practical Suggestion No.4
## Appreciate Others!

A neighbour who greets you with a bright smile and cheerful hello...

A thank you card from a friend who was pleased and touched by your gift...

A box of chocolates which your spouse brings home to you...

A warm, delicious and wholesome meal that your mother has cooked and kept ready for you...

A friend who asks you with genuine care and concern, " How are you?"...

Every day we are witness to acts of loving kindness offered to us. Let us not dismiss them as small or trivial. They deserve to be appreciated!

It is our besetting fault that we often take others for granted. We eat what is placed on the table but fail to appreciate the person who cooked the meal.

We lean on our friends for support, cry on their shoulders but fail to appreciate them for always *being there* for us.

Silent gratitude is not of much use to anyone. Therefore, learn to express your appreciation. It is not enough to *think* that someone is being kind and good; a kind word unsaid is a kind thought wasted. Go up to people, reach out to praise them, thank them, appreciate them for what they have done and you will really make a difference!

I knew a young man who came from a wealthy family of successful businessmen. Unfortunately for him, being born with the proverbial silver spoon did not do him much good emotionally. His parents were convinced that the only way to make him achieve success was to criticise him constantly. He had to learn! He had to avoid making mistakes! He needed to be told what was wrong with him. Life was tough. It was a big, bad world out there and he had to be aware that there was a rat race which he had to win at all costs. And so they constantly criticised him; they found fault with everything he did. He had to get better! He had to try harder! His efforts were not good enough for them, no matter how hard he tried!

The young man did succeed. He too became a successful wealthy entrepreneur, just like his father. But he was not a happy man. He regarded his work as a severe drudgery; he was always conscious of the mistakes he made; he was constantly depressed; he undervalued himself. He was scarred for life because he had failed to receive appreciation when he needed it!

Ludwig Van Bethoven was one of the greatest musicians the world has known. At the age of 11 he began to compose his music and in his teens he won fame and fortune as a great composer.

One evening, Beethoven was passing a cobbler's cottage, when he heard someone practising one of his compositions. As he paused to listen, he heard a girl exclaim, "I wish I could hear a real musician playing this piece, so that I could learn to render it properly!"

Beethoven entered the cottage and found a young girl seated at a piano. She was blind. Offering to play for her, he sat at the piano and played for an hour or so.

The girl was enthralled! Her appreciation fired the enthusiasm of Beethoven, and he went on playing.

Dusk had set in; the cottage grew dark but the silvery moonlight filtered into the room. Under its inspiration and the whole-hearted warmth of the girl's appreciation, Beethoven composed his famous *Moonlight Sonata!*

Not all of us are blessed with great musical talent, or a captivating voice. Not all of us have what are called 'leadership qualities' or 'organising abilities'. We don't all win prizes, awards and scholarships. But all of us can and must cultivate the beautiful quality of appreciation. We must learn to praise others. It is no mean thing to possess this special talent for praising others, for without our appreciation, the brightest people in the world cannot shine!

Ask any famous singer: can he give a concert in an empty hall?

Ask an actor: what would he be without his fans?

Ask a writer: whom is he writing for?

Appreciation works wonders. And don't think this is confined to spiritual matters alone; it works in every field, every walk of life.

A distinguished professor of the Kelloggs Business School, Deepak Jain, observes: "A leader will be truly successful only when his subordinates believe that they can grow under him."

How best can this impression be conveyed to them? Surely by the leader's words of appreciation and encouragement!

There was a multimillionaire who prided himself on never wasting time with unnecessary things. He never offered a tip for any services; nor did he even bother to appreciate anyone for the help rendered to him.

His complicated finances had all been handled by his chief accountant, a man who had served him faithfully for decades. One day, the accountant committed suicide. The millionaire was devastated. Where would he ever find anyone who was so committed, so sincere, so trustworthy?

The cash transactions and account books were found to be in perfect order, for the dead man was a meticulous worker. He had also left a brief note for his employer, which read: "In 30 years of working for you, I have never heard one word of encouragement from you. You must be very proud of that!"

If only parents, leaders, managers, bosses and husbands administered much needed doses of appreciation and encouragement, we would no longer have people who suffer from inferiority complex.

A father brought his twin boys to a counsellor who specialised in dealing with difficult children. "Tom is bright and intelligent," he informed the psychiatrist, "but David seems quite inferior, mentally and physically. I wish you would talk to the boy and find out what is wrong with him."

The psychiatrist worked hard to gain the little boy's confidence, putting him at ease and drawing him out gradually. What he finally told the doctor was indeed revealing.

"People don't seem to like me," the boy mused. "Whenever my brother does something, mama and papa smile. When I do anything, they scowl. I can't ever seem to do anything as good as he does!"

The doctor understood his problem. He advised the parents to separate the boys as far as possible and never to compare one with the other unfavourably. They were also put in different schools. The little boy's parents were asked to praise him for his own accomplishments. It made all the difference to him!

All of us need to bask in the warmth of appreciation every now and then. Otherwise, our self-respect becomes endangered.

A young man who was about to begin his career was told by his father, " You must learn to give your best with or without appreciation. Don't let the quality of your work suffer because others do not praise you."

Sound words indeed. It is good *not to expect* appreciation for all that we do. But surely, nothing stops us from expressing our appreciation for others! Now for example, if the young man's bosses had been told, "Don't be content with just paying your workers salary. Encourage them with your words of appreciation whenever possible!" – what a world of difference it would have made to the young man's work!

Perhaps husbands are more insensitive, more lacking in this aspect than their wives. A survey of women in rural America revealed that the wives of the farmers had one common complaint; they were taken for granted. They were hardly ever thanked for what they did.

One of them narrated an amusing incident. Every day she took the trouble to make a delicious meal for her husband and sons, when they returned home in the evening. She learnt new recipes. She prepared complicated dishes. It was obvious that they enjoyed the meal for it disappeared in no time at all. But not a word of thanks, not a single compliment was forthcoming.

In exasperation, she made a meal of cattle feed and set it, steaming hot, on the table one evening.

"What's this?" they screamed, when they had downed the first mouthful, "Are you crazy or what?"

"I have waited 26 years and not heard a word of praise from you," she replied. "I never ever thought that you would notice the difference."

A lady was invited to spend Christmas with her wealthy cousins. She was taken aback at the voluminous heap of presents around the tree, for this family loved to give away gifts and several gifts at a time, to one another.

Christmas morning was just a riot of ripping open parcels and looking at the multiple gifts. The lady also had her fair share. But she saw that while there was a flood of presents there was no *presence*. "Mounds of merchandise were ripped open," she wrote. " But no sense of true appreciation was expressed or revealed."

What a gap between material plenty and emotional lack!

The Sufi Saint Jami tells us: "We can spend a whole lifetime enjoying various benefits and not appreciate their value until we are deprived of them."

How very true! Only when something is over, or someone is gone, do we realise how much we appreciated – but failed to express what they meant to us! And then we are weighed down by the negative force of "if only…"

Many years ago, a famous singer was contracted to perform at a Paris Opera House. The announcements of the programme were made months in advance. Expectedly the programme was a sell-out.

On the appointed night, the auditorium was packed to capacity. The richest and most powerful men and women of Paris were eager and waiting to hear the celebrated singer.

The theatre manager appeared on stage. "Ladies and gentlemen," he began, "We thank you for your tremendous enthusiasm and support. I regret to inform you that our star singer cannot appear before you, as she is unwell. However, we have a substitute, who we are sure will provide you with good entertainment."

An audible groan emanated from the crowd. Their faces fell, they murmured their disappointment and frustration. No one even caught the name of the singer.

She sang beautifully indeed! She did all she could, she gave of her best. But when the performance was over, only a stony silence greeted her. The crowd had so forgotten its manners that they failed to give her an applause.

Then, a little voice was heard from the balcony. A small girl stood up and shouted, "Mama! I think you are wonderful!"

The audience were shamed into a response. In unison they all arose and gave the singer a standing ovation!

Every now and then, all of us need to hear someone say the same to *us*, "I think you are wonderful!" And *we* need to say this to our friends, our colleagues and co-workers, our parents, spouses and children.

Why don't *you* utter these magic words of appreciation to someone today?

The popular comedian Jimmy Durante was entertaining a packed auditorium of wounded soldiers in a Stanton Island War Hospital. The soldiers were so appreciative that there were several 'encores' at the end of the programme.

During those thunderous ovations and applause, Durante's secretary kept on making anxious signals to the actor. They had to leave for New York as soon as possible – for he had two very important programmes scheduled there the next day.

Durante noticed his desperate signals and mouthed a silent NO. He pointed to his secretary two wounded soldiers in the front row, who were laughing heartily and enjoying the show thoroughly. Each one of them had an arm amputated – and they were clapping with their remaining hands, one on the other.

"I have never received such an appreciation in my life!" Durante whispered.

He went on to entertain the wounded soldiers throughout the night.

Encouragement is activated by expressing appreciation. It is not enough to think how good someone is. We have got to tell them what we feel. After all, people cannot read our minds! We must not be like the young man who says to his wife, "Honey, when I sit down and think about how much you mean to me, I can hardly keep myself from telling you so!"

Silent appreciation is of no use to anyone! Don't keep it to yourself! As Dale Carnegie tells us: "Three-fourths of the people you will ever meet are hungering and thirsting for appreciation. Give it to them and they will love you!" Indeed, appreciative words are the greatest incentive for doing good work.

When you tell your child, husband or friend that they are wrong, that they are insensitive or that they have done something badly, you take away their incentive for improvement. On the other hand, when you are liberal with your encouragement and appreciation, they will do their best and surprise you with what they can achieve!

I read about a boy who had been naughty. During family prayers that night, the father specifically prayed for his son, mentioning a number of bad things the boy had done.

The six-year old began to sob. "Daddy always tells God all the bad things about me!" he cried. "He never tells him the good things I do!"

Making others feel good about themselves builds better relationships. This is what Lord Chesterfield urges his son to do: make every person like himself a little better, and he or she will begin to like you very much. Sincere praise reassures people. It dissolves the negative notions they have about themselves and improves their self-esteem.

It was George Mathew Adams who said: "He who appreciates another, enriches himself far more than the one whom he praises. To praise is an investment in one's own happiness. The poorest human being has something to give that the richest could not buy."

Let me share with you a lovely incident narrated by a teacher. In the junior class that she taught, there were two boys named Ted. One was well-behaved, hard-working and intelligent. The other was a sluggard, difficult to control and a constant nuisance in class.

The young teacher sighed everytime she caught sight of the second Ted. She was convinced that he was going to be a problem child who would blight this – the first year of her life as a teacher.

Towards the end of the term, a PTA meeting was held. A pleasant and well-dressed mother came up to the teacher and asked her, "How's my son Ted doing?"

Looking at the mother, the young teacher just assumed that she was the 'good' Ted's mother. She answered enthusiastically, "He's a lovely child! I must say I enjoy having him in my class!"

The mother beamed. "I'm so glad to hear that," she said gratefully.

The next morning 'problem' Ted came up to the teacher in class. "My mom told me what you said about me at the PTA meeting last night." He swallowed hard. "I don't think any teacher has ever liked me, or said nice things about me before!"

Ted was a different boy altogether from then on. He stopped being naughty. His work was done systematically. There were several occasions when the teacher had ample opportunity to praise him genuinely. Each time, he glowed with pride and happiness – and improved further! It was not long before the problem boy became one of the best students in class.

Perhaps the incident of mistaken identity was meant to teach the young teacher a valuable lesson: genuine appreciation can work wonders! A sound investment in praise and trust can indeed reap rich dividends. And when we enrich the lives of others, we enrich our own!

Couples who have enjoyed happy, successful marriages have one thing in common, whoever they are, wherever they may live: they *work hard* to make their marriage a success; and they never ever take each other for granted. It is not enough for the husband to say, "Of course I appreciate my wife and she knows it." It is not enough for the wife to say, "My husband knows I love him." She/he probably knows it; but it makes a lot of difference when you actually say it out aloud.

Once I addressed a large gathering in Hong Kong where I urged the husbands in the audience to express their appreciation for their wives. "When you go home tonight," I said to them, "just tell your wife these seven, simple words: *Honey, where would I be without you?"*

The following day, a woman came to see me. She said to me with tears in her eyes, "I have been married for 35 years. Yesterday, for the first time ever, my husband told me how much he appreciated and loved me. He said that you had urged him to express himself. I want you to know how much this means to me."

*Honey, where would I be without you?* Seems very easy to say, doesn't it? In fact, we could say it several times a day – but we don't!

Sometimes people learn to appreciate something valuable only when they have lost it. There was a man who was a highly paid executive in a multinational company. He and his family enjoyed a high standard of living – a big, beautiful, apartment, a luxury car, holidays abroad, etc.

They took it all for granted – until one day, the company decided to retrench its staff, and the man lost his job.

At first, he was not unduly worried. He was not only highly qualified, but well-experienced. He assumed he could walk into a job very soon. But that was not to be. It was a period of industrial recession, and he was unable to find a suitable position, hard as he tried.

Amidst the hardship and anxiety, a thought crossed his mind: as long as he was well off, he had never really appreciated what he had – plenty of money, facilities, and all the good things of life. Nor had he ever thought of showing his gratitude to God for it all, by sharing his wealth with others. He had never really learnt to give, to share and care.

Then and there he resolved that when he found another job, he would be more appreciative of God's grace. He would set aside some of his earnings to be spent in the service of those less fortunate than himself. He would take nothing for granted.

Within a few weeks, he had found a job. But he was a changed man now. He expressed his gratitude to God and resolved that he would live a life that would bear witness to his appreciation of all the blessings he had received.

Appreciation is like a light that brightens up life. It is like a tonic that invigorates and energises people. Like a ray of light that strikes crystal, its brightness is reflected back to you.

When you feel the impulse to appreciate something or someone, I urge you to do it right away; otherwise the impulse will fade, and your appreciation will remain unexpressed. Just think of the number of times you have thought of sending a thank you card, making a phone call or paying a compliment – and then forgot all about it! Therefore, when you feel like appreciating someone, do it right away!

A scientist was attending a conference in Delhi. He was offered the chance to make a presentation to the conference, as one of the paper readers had not turned up. Though he had all the matter he needed, he was in a urgent need of expert assistance on the computer, so that he could accompany his presentation with effective visual aids. He located a small computer centre with printing facilities near his hotel, and went in to enquire if they could assist him. To his pleasant surprise it was staffed by polite, enthusiastic young men and women who agreed to do all that he required. On the evening before his presentation, they stayed back till 11.00 p.m. at night putting together the material for his paper. There was a hefty bill to pay, but he was only too happy to pay it – they deserved it, he said to himself.

His paper was very well received – and the accompanying computer graphics were especially appreciated by everyone, including the international delegates. His paper was declared to be the best one at the conference – even though he had been asked to present it only as a stopgap arrangement!

That evening, as he returned to his hotel, he thought of the young staff members at the computer centre, and his heart was filled with deep appreciation. He bought a box of chocolates from the hotel's gift shop and walked round to the computer centre.

"Hello Sir!" the manager called out cheerfully on seeing him. " How did your presentation go?"

"It went off very well indeed," beamed the scientist. "And I'm here to say thank you to everyone of you!"

He unwrapped the gaily decorated box and offered it to each one. They exchanged glances at each other as they accepted the delicious chocolates. One of the girls said, "Sir, we have worked on dozens of presentations, dozens of student projects, company reports and several Ph.D. dissertations. We have always done our best for our customers. But no one has ever bought chocolates to say thank you to us! Your gesture is just wonderful!"

He could not have pleased them so much even if he had given them money! And, as we all know, lots of things in life are more important than money!

There is an old lady who is the seniormost resident in her housing society. Every morning at six, as she leaves for her daily walk with her husband, she prepares a flask of tea, which she passes on to the security guards at the gates of the society. It does not matter who happens to be on duty – they can count on their early morning cup of tea from her!

"Madam, how kind of you to think of us and offer us this much needed cup of tea!" one of the security guards said to her.

"Well, we sleep in peace every night, because you guys are on duty," she smiled. "The tea is just my small way of showing my appreciation to you!"

Does your son/daughter work in shifts at a call centre or BPO? Try to give him/her sufficient rest and relaxation whenever they are home. Make sure you express your love and appreciation of their hard work.

Does your husband have a stressful job? Help him unwind when he comes home exhausted. Make him feel welcome, wanted and loved. Do not pour out all your complaints to him as soon as he sets foot inside the house.

Is your wife a working woman? Don't expect her to tackle the cooking and the household chores single-handed, *and* wait on the family members hand and foot *and* bring home her salary every month. Show your appreciation by helping her in the kitchen, and share the household tasks with her.

A mother and wife who runs the home, does the cooking, cleaning and washing, attends to the children and handles visitors and guests, is perhaps even busier than an executive in a company – show your appreciation to your mother/wife with words and gestures!

Expressing appreciation is the best way to bring a glow in someone's heart – and you are sure to feel its warmth in your heart too!

---

Give a grateful man more than he asks.

*– Portuguese proverb*

---

# Practical Suggestion No. 5
## Walk with God Today – Trust Him for the Morrow

Trust in the goodness and caring power of the Lord! My beloved Master, Sadhu Vaswani, said to us again and again, "God upsets our plans to set up His own – and His plans are perfect."

A child has absolute trust and faith in his mother. Have you ever heard of a baby worrying over where his next feed of milk is going to come from? He knows he has his mother near – and therefore nothing to fear.

If such is the trust that a child reposes in his human parent, how much more trust should we place in the loving care of God, the Divine Father and Mother to all of us! God is all love and all wisdom. He is too loving to punish, too wise to make a mistake. Therefore, trust in His goodness, live in the faith that in everything that happens to you, there is the profound meaning of His mercy.

There is a lovely little parable that tells us of two little birds, a robin and a sparrow, who were watching the mad whirl of the world of men around them.

"Tell me cousin," said the robin to the sparrow, "I should really like to know why these poor human beings rush about and worry so."

The sparrow replied, "Perhaps these poor people have no heavenly Father who cares for them, like the One who cares for you and me!"

A devout Christian pilgrim undertook a walking tour of the Holy Land around Jerusalem. He came across a shepherd with whom he struck up a conversation.

The old shepherd showed the staff he carried and explained that it was something that had been done in Palestine for thousands of years. "This staff is meant to comfort my sheep," he asserted.

"How can your staff comfort the sheep?" asked the puzzled pilgrim.

"During the day, I carry my staff across the shoulders – the sheep see it and they know I am here," he said. "At night, when the hills are covered in mist and we cannot see where we are, I tap with my staff on the ground and my sheep know that I am near."

The pilgrim was thrilled! Surely this was what David had meant when he said: "It would be unreasonable to suppose that God has less care for me than I had for the sheep!" He thought with tear-filled eyes of the beautiful lines:

Ye, though I walk through the valley of the shadow of death,
I will fear no evil, for Thou art with me; Thy rod and Thy staff, they comfort me.

During the blitz in London, a number of people had sought refuge in a dark and confined air-raid shelter. It was a cold and miserable night, and they huddled together in misery, unable to sleep a wink.

Among them was an old lady, who snuggled into her blanket and fell asleep contentedly.

When she woke up after the all-clear siren, they asked her, "How could you sleep amidst all the tension and discomfort?"

"I said my prayers to God before I went to sleep," she said. "Where's the need for both Him and me to keep awake?"

God can take care of us in darkness and light, storm and sunshine.

Three children were left alone in a cottage, while their parents had gone out to work in the fields. Suddenly a terrible storm broke out, and thunder, lightning and rain lashed the small house.

The two older children were terrified and began to scream in terror. "What will become of us?" they wailed. "Surely, surely, we are going to be washed away in the deluge!"

"Stop crying!" ordered the youngest. "Don't you suppose God knows His business?"

A ragged little urchin used to come to pray at a small wayside temple every morning, before he set off on his daily work, which was rag picking.

A lady who met him at the temple every morning, once asked the boy, "You pray to God so devoutly every day. Why does He not take better care of you? Why can't He tell someone to give you decent clothes, good food and a better livelihood?"

The little boy's face fell. But he cheered up in an instant and said to her, " I guess God does tell someone – but obviously that someone keeps forgetting."

The lady was so touched by the simple faith of the little boy that she resolved that *she* would be the one who would help him with all the things she had mentioned!

Two children were playing on a hillside, as sunset approached. Mesmerised by the brilliant colours of the western sky, they stopped what they were doing and gazed in wonder.

"Look how fast the sun has travelled!" exclaimed the first. "Just a short while ago, it was above that tree, and now, it's low down in the sky."

"It isn't the sun that is moving," exclaimed her companion. "It is the earth. That's what my father told me."

The first girl shook her head. "I *saw* the sun moving," she said stubbornly. "And I *know* the earth did not move, because I have been standing on it all the time."

They argued for a while, and the first one insisted, "I know what I see."

"And I believe my father!" was her friend's response.

This is how mankind is divided – some of us accepting only what their senses reveal to them, the others implicitly trusting their Heavenly Father.

John Wesley who founded the Quakers' Movement was once walking with a troubled man, who had great misgivings about the love and goodness of God. "How can He leave me in so much worry and trouble?" he kept asking repeatedly.

Just then they came across a cow looking over a stone wall. "Do you know why that cow is looking over the wall?" asked Wesley.

"No," said the man.

Wesley said, "The cow is looking *over* the wall because she cannot see *through* it. That is what you must do with your wall of trouble – look over it."

Trust in the Lord enables us to transcend circumstances and look over the wall of worry and mistrust.

There is an old English custom which is still practised by sailors in some parts of England. When a ship is about to sail, the captain asks all the assembled sailors, "Are we all here?"

"Yes sir," they reply.

"Are we all ready to sail?"

"Yes sir – in God's care," is the answer.

"So, have we anything to fear then?" he continues.

"No sir, nothing!" is the answer.

Then they set sail, unafraid of the many dangers which still beset men who live on the sea and by the sea.

What an inspiring practice this is! I am reminded of some beautiful lines that I read somewhere –

> He knows, He loves, He cares,
> Nothing this truth can dim,
> He does the very best for those
> Who leave the choice with Him.

God's love exhorts us to cast away all our cares, and keep our faith and confidence in Him. Alas, being folk of little faith, we do just the opposite – we cast away our confidence and cling to our cares!

It is said that God brings down a curtain of darkness every night – so that we can shut off the day that is past and start afresh on the morrow. Sir William Osler, the famous Victorian physician, suggested that we should also pull down our mental curtains every night – and shut out the disappointments of the past or anxieties about the future.

Just stop to think for a minute: suppose you knew that this is your last day on earth, how would you choose to spend those precious last hours of your life? When you answer that question, you will have answered how you *ought to live* everyday of your life.

God takes care of you today, as He cared for you in the past, and will care for you in the future. Stop brooding over the past and worrying about tomorrow.

During the blitz of World War II, a father rushed out from a building that had just been struck by a bomb. He was holding his little girl by the hand, and had to get to a shelter as soon as possible, so that they would not be hit. But the nearest air raid shelter was far away!

In front of them was a gaping hole in the ground which had been left by a large shell explosion several days earlier. With the German bombers still flying overhead, the father lost no time. He jumped into the hole and held up his arms for his young daughter to follow.

Terrified by the explosions and fires all around her, and, unable to see her father in the darkness of the hole, she sobbed, "But I can't see you papa!"

The father looked up at the night sky lit with the tracer lights of the aircraft and by the red glow of burning buildings. He called out to his little girl, whose silhouette showed clearly at the hole's edge, "But I can see you clearly my darling! Jump!"

The little girl jumped – not because she could see her father, but because she trusted him implicitly to do the best for her.

We may not always see where our Heavenly Father is leading us – but we can trust Him absolutely! His ever-protecting arms and ever-lasting care are always there for us!

A little cabin boy was polishing the deck of the ship, when the captain called out to him, "Boy, can you climb?"

"Yes captain," said the boy, who was thrilled to be noticed by the captain, for he hoped to be a sailor when he grew up. "I used to climb the highest trees in my village."

In those days, sailing ships had huge masts. At the captain's bidding, the lad climbed the main mast in a trice, with great dexterity and agility. He was almost at the top when he looked down and began to feel dizzy.

"O captain! I am seasick! I am sure I am going to fall down! Help, oh help!" he cried.

"Look up my boy, look up!" called the captain.

The boy did as he was told. The sight of the blue sky was calm and reassuring. The dangerous dizziness vanished and his fears dissolved.

Looking up to God is the act of faith that can reassure us at all times!

Wise men appreciate all men, for they see the good in each and know how hard it is to make anything good.

*— Baltasar Gracian*

## Practical Suggestion No. 6
## Let the Words 'Thank You God!' Be on Your Lips Constantly

Let me begin this section by narrating to you a beautiful incident from the life of my beloved Master, Sadhu Vaswani.

It was an early hour of the morning. The first flutings of birds had died, and many of them, with wings outstretched, were flying in the skies. In our small garden, flowers smiled and the green leaves of shrubs and trees glistened in the first rays of the morning sun. All nature appeared gay, beautiful as a bride on her wedding day. But my heart was sad.

Sadhu Vaswani lay ill, in great pain. He had passed a restless night and though his eyelids were heavy with slumber, the shooting pains all over his body would not let him sleep for more than a few minutes at a time.

I watched over him throughout the night and had seen how, even when the pain was very acute, he continued to smile a smile radiant as the star-lit skies of Sind. When the pain became unbearable, out of his parted lips came the one-word song, *"Shukur! Shukur!"* (Gratitude to Thee, O Lord of mercy!)

Sadhu Vaswani's feeble body was so broken with illness and pain that it was a wonder how he could bear it. I also wondered that this man of purity and prayer, service and sacrifice, this man who would not hurt an ant and who gave the love of his gentle, generous heart to all, the rich and the poor, the young and the old, the sinner and the saint – and who loved birds and animals and every flower of the field and every lotus in the lake and every atom of matter and every ray of light – I wondered that such a man should have to suffer so terribly?

Through Sadhu Vaswani, healing flowed to many who were sick and afflicted; now when he himself was in the throes of pain, nothing could be done to give him relief! The doctors were helpless, and we, who were near him, could only wake and watch and shed tears of sorrow! Such is the way of those who would be the saviours and servers, the helpers and healers of humanity!

At about three o'clock in the night, finding it difficult to bear the sight of his suffering, I said to him, "Beloved! You are a friend of God. Why will you not pray to Him that He may give you healing?"

Sadhu Vaswani smiled again as he answered: "To me, my child, there is nothing holier than the Will of the Lord. And if it be His Will that I suffer, such suffering is sweeter to me than relief from pain. Verily, in the fulfilment of His Holy Will is my real comfort and solace!"

After a brief while, with uplifted eyes, he prayed, "Gratitude to Thee, my God and my Lord, for this gift of pain! And if it be Thy Will to add to it tenfold, I pray Thee to do so without delay. In Thy Will is the peace I seek!"

And I recalled how the great woman-mystic, Rabia, being urged by a friend to pray for relief from illness, answered: "Do you not know who it is that wills this suffering for me? Is it not God who wills it? Why, then, do you bid me ask for what is contrary to His Will? It is not well to oppose one's Beloved!"

There is a lovely prayer taught to little children in Nursery classes. We would all do well to recite it daily:

Thank you God for the world so sweet:
Thank you God for the food we eat:
Thank you God for the birds that sing:
Thank you God for everything!

Do you thank God when you sit down to eat your food? Do you pause to think of the many people who have put in their effort, their hard work to make the hot, delicious, meal on your plate a reality? The farmers who till the field and sow the crop; the men and women who harvest and bind the grain; the miller who processes the grain; the merchants who clean and package it; the grocers and green grocers who bring your chosen items into the market; and the person or persons who transform all the raw ingredients into an appetising meal that is placed before you? And, above all God who makes this miraculous process an every day event in the world?

I am sure you have all heard of the little boy who was invited out to lunch at a neighbour's house. When everybody was seated at the table, delicious, piping hot dishes were served and everyone began to eat heartily.

The little boy asked with a puzzled expression on his face, "Don't you say 'thank you' before you eat?"

"No, not really," mumbled his host, with his mouth full. "Where's the time for all that?"

The boy nodded wisely and reflected for a minute. "My dog is like you! He starts to eat right away!"

I am reminded of the words of the great Sikh Guru, Guru Arjan Dev, in that immortal classic – the *Sukhmani* from which we recite every day. *Kartoot pashu ke maanush zaat,* says the Guru. We wear human faces, but our actions and deeds are like those of animals!

The ancients believed that there were three levels of life in man – the divine, the human and the animal. We can rise to the divine, when we aspire to it. Most of the times, we are just human. But we should guard against sinking as low as the level of the beast.

A human being is one who thanks God for every favour he receives!

Let me suggest a simple prayer of thanksgiving which you can offer whenever you sit down to a meal:

This food, O Lord, I offer unto Thee! Touch it as Thy *prasadam* and return it to me. And so bless me Lord, that every ounce of energy that I get out of this food may be spent in Thy service, in the service of the poor and broken ones, in the service of birds and animals, who are my younger brothers in the one family of Creation. Lord! Thou hast given me food for the body; grant me also sustenance for the soul. And bless everyone of those without whose help this food could not have reached this table.

Do not labour under the delusion that gratitude is meant only for the high and the mighty. It gladdens the heart of everyone who receives it!

Cicero was a well-known philosopher and orator in ancient Rome. Not only was he a great teacher, but also a highly sought after guest in the elite society of Rome.

One day, he was invited to dine at the house of a student. When he arrived there, the entire household was elated. Here was a celebrity, a great philosopher and respected statesman, who had honoured them by accepting their humble invitation! As for the servants in the house, they were overawed by the presence of the god-like guest.

When the meal was over, Cicero thanked every member of his host's family. He then turned to the bearers who had served the meal and said to them, "Thank you! The food was indeed delicious, but it was rendered more tasty by your wonderful service!"

The slaves were in tears. No one had ever thanked them so graciously before!

There was an old lady who dearly loved the Lord. Her favourite expression was, "Thanks to the Almighty!" Wherever she was, in the midst of a congregation, or at a feast gathering, she would break out into her joyous shout, "Thanks to the Almighty!"

The minister at the local church was often startled out of his wits when "Aunt Betty" uttered her clarion call in the midst of his sermon. One day, he called her and told her that he would give her a pair of blankets if only she would refrain from saying, "Thanks to the Almighty," loudly – during the service.

Now he knew that she desperately needed those blankets, for she was very poor indeed. For two Sundays together, she kept quiet during the sermon. She was doing her best to 'earn' the blankets on the minister's terms.

On the third Sunday, a visiting minister was to preach at their church. His discourse was so inspiring that Aunt Betty forgot all about her earthly reward and sprang up out of her pew to cry, "Blankets or no blankets, Thanks to the Almighty!"

A group of friends met for an informal meal. They had several memories to share, much news to exchange, lots of information to catch up.

As the evening shadows lengthened, one of them asked, "Can you tell me – each of you – which was the best day of your life?"

"The day I was married!" said a young wife, in whose eyes the stars of romance were still shining.

"The day my first child was born!" exclaimed a mother. "I felt myself blessed that day!"

"The day I was fired from my first job," laughed a successful entrepreneur. "I decided to throw it all up and start a business of my own. It was the best decision I ever made."

And so it went on, until it was the turn of a young lady who had not spoken a word. "Which was the best day of *your* life?" they asked her.

She answered, "The best day of my life is *today* – because it is the day that I value the most. After all, I can't get back yesterday, and I am not sure of tomorrow. This day is mine, to make it into whatever

I want it to be. And because it's new and I am alive in it, it's *the best* and I thank God for it!"

Whatever the condition in which we find ourselves, whatever be the suffering through which we pass, let us thank the Lord constantly! When we do so, our hearts expand and we become receptive to the helpful and healing forces of God.

An aged lady was travelling to see her daughter who lived in a distant town. Part of her journey was across a river which she had to cross by a country boat. A terrible storm broke as they were crossing, and the passengers huddled together, calling upon God to help them, protect them and save their lives.

The old lady sat in a corner, unconcerned. Her lips only muttered the words, "Praise be to the Lord!"

When the storm had subsided, her fellow passengers asked her how she managed to remain so calm.

"It's like this," she explained. "I have two daughters. One of them is dead, and I believe she is in Heaven. The other lives in the village down the river. When the storm arose, I only wondered which daughter I would visit. I would have loved to see either one! And so I only had thanks to give to the Lord!"

In every situation and circumstance of life, let us utter the one word of gratitude, *"Shukur! Shukur! Shukur!"*

Of a Sufi *dervish* it is said that one day, as he was taking a bath in the river, he was bitten in the foot by a crocodile. Blood flowed from the wound. He swam with great difficulty to the river-bank where he lay, uttering the words of praise, *"Shukur! Shukur! Shukur!"*

A man who watched the whole scene was amazed. "You are bleeding profusely and you must be in great pain!" he exclaimed. "Yet you still say, *Shukur! Shukur! Shukur!* What do you have to thank the Lord for?"

The *dervish* answered calmly, "I feel grateful to God that I fell into the mouth of the crocodile, I did not fall into the mouth of sin!"

There was a man of true faith!

The man of faith knows that God is the controller of his destiny – indeed, the controller of the entire cosmos. All that happens anywhere in the universe is controlled by God. And God, as I have stressed repeatedly, is loving and wise. So, the man of faith lives in the faith that all that happens, happens for the best. He resists nothing, he expects nothing and he rejoices in all that happens to him. He is never on the defensive. He never ever feels isolated or alone.

In every condition, every circumstance of life, let these words come out of the very depths of our hearts, "Thank you God! Thank you God!" We will find that we are filled with a peace that will amaze us. When we thank the Lord all the time, we build for ourselves a ladder of consciousness on which we can climb and touch the very pinnacle of peace.

Of course, there are bound to be several people who would argue, "How is it possible to say, "thank you God," all the time? Just look at the world we live in! It's a terrible place. Consider the times we live in – these are troubled and disturbing times. And we are confronted by problems wherever we turn!"

My answer to them is this, "God has faith in us, and He knows that troubles can make us better, stronger human beings."

It is so easy to add up our troubles – but it takes some effort to focus on things which we ought to be grateful for. So, even when we are overwhelmed by problems, let us focus our minds on positive things and thank God for all the wonderful things of life –

family and friends, sunshine, stars and sky. Let us thank Him too, for sufferings and disappointments – for they make us evolve spiritually.

A special service programme was being organised at the *ashram* of a holy man. The parents of a brave young soldier, who had been killed in action, had donated a generous amount for a memorial *seva* to be conducted to honour his sacrifice. Parents of his colleagues were also attending the prayer meeting that preceded the *seva*.

When the announcement of the service programme was made, one of the mothers whispered to her husband, "Let us do the same for our boy!"

"What are you saying?" demanded the husband. "Our son is still alive! He didn't lose his life!"

"That's just the point," said the mother, with tears in her eyes. "Let us give what we can, in gratitude to the Lord, for sparing his life!"

The poet George Herbert prayed: "Our Father, Thou hast given us so much. Give us one more thing – a grateful heart!"

A New York postal employee found that in the months before Christmas, thousands of letters were addressed to Santa Claus – letters written by people asking for something. But in the months that followed Christmas, only *one* card arrived, thanking Santa for his gifts. How quick we are to ask and receive! How slow we are to spread the magic word – *Thank you!*

At a Question-Answer session, a young girl asked me, "Dada, you talk of the chains of desire by which all of us are bound. Can you tell me how I may break these fetters and free myself?"

I said to her: "The simplest way to break those fetters is to thank God for all that He sends you. By doing so you accept His Will and release yourself from the bondage of desires."

When you accept all that comes your way and rejoice in all that happens to you, you thank God and offer Him praise. You expect nothing; you hope for nothing; you need nothing; you lack nothing. You will be the happiest person on earth!

The French poet, Lamartine, was taking a walk in a poor quarter of the city when he came across a humble stonecutter at work. The poet was surprised to hear him utter the words, "Thank you God!" after each stroke of the hammer.

"My good man, whom are you thanking?" enquired the poet haughtily. "And what are you thanking Him for? Had you been wealthy and prosperous, it would be natural for you to thank God. But God thought of you just once when He made you – and hasn't remembered you since, for He has left you to a hard and tough life!"

"I thank God that He remembered a poor stonecutter *once!* That's nothing to be sneezed at! Thank you God, thank you!" exclaimed the man.

Such is the spirit of true gratitude!

> No duty is more urgent than that of returning thanks.
>
> *– Saint Ambrose*
>
> If a fellow isn't thankful for what he's got, he isn't likely to be thankful for what he's going to get.
>
> *– Frank A Clark*

## Practical Suggestion No. 7
## Thank God – Even When the Going is Tough!

It is so easy for us to thank God when everything is going well for us. Life seems to be moving, it seems to be moving on well-oiled wheels, as it were.

Sant Kabir has a different viewpoint: "Everyone remembers God during misery, but forgets Him when there is prosperity. If one were to remember God in prosperity, there would not be any misery for him."

This is true, for when we are afflicted with pain and suffering, we seek God's help in desperation. We feel that He cannot hear us. We imagine that He doesn't care! We berate Him for being indifferent to our suffering.

But I am talking of a state beyond calling upon God – I am asking you to actually *thank* God for adversity, suffering and pain.

The trouble with many of us is that we remember God with great alacrity in our misery – but the moment our problems are sorted out, we cease to think of Him. Thus, we have just used God; we have treated Him as if He were just a means to serve our end.

There is a humorous story told to us about such a man who turned to God in desperation.

A childless man went to the temple and made a sacred vow before Lord Shiva. "O Lord! just give me a son, and I shall offer you five hundred rupees!"

The man's prayer was answered. His wife gave birth to a bonny baby boy. The man's joy knew no bounds.

He remembered his vow, of course; he remembered it very well indeed!

Everyday he said to himself, "Now I must offer five hundred rupees to Lord Shiva." Or, "I shall give it soon." "I must give it … I shall give it."

Soon, he began to change his mind. He thought, "What a trifle my money must be to Lord Shiva! He is the King of all the three worlds! Everything in the world belongs to Him. Five hundred is the same as fifty to Him. So I shall offer Him fifty rupees."

Gradually it dawned on him that the best offering was not rupees but coconuts.

He went to a coconut seller and asked for five coconuts. As it was not the season for coconuts, he was told, "You can have five coconuts for ten rupees."

The man was horrified. "Two rupees for each coconut?" he exclaimed. "Give me five for five rupees!"

"Why don't you go and ask the farmer in the coconut grove?" said the shopkeeper. "He may be willing to sell you five coconuts for five rupees."

The coconut grove was far away.

By the time he got there, the man said to himself, "I have walked all the way here and my chappals are quite worn out. I must get five coconuts for three rupees from the farmer."

But the farmer was adamant. "If you want the coconuts so cheap, you must climb the tree and pluck them yourself."

The man was delighted with this bargain. Without even thinking, he began to climb the tree. Never having done it before, he slipped and fell; quite a few of his bones were broken. He had to be hospitalised for several days. The doctor's bill far exceeded the five hundred rupees he had vowed to offer to the Lord.

I often tell my friends that joy and sorrow are both essential to light the rainbow sky of human life. Our life is as much ennobled by adversity as it is enriched by joy. If all of us were content and complacent in our prosperity, there would be no progress – material or spiritual success. Growth and spiritual evolution depend upon very special qualities like perseverance, tolerance, endurance, and tenacity. It is adversity that helps us develop these 'spiritual muscles'.

Speaking from the spiritual point of view, adversities and disappointments are meant to strengthen our resolve, test our faith and enhance our determination to move Godward.

A football team was on its way to a crucial game in the league. They were travelling by train, when a reporter boarded their carriage and asked to speak to the coach.

"Is it true that you always take with you a chaplain to pray for the victory of the team?" asked the reporter. "Could I meet him please?"

"Certainly," replied the coach, "Which one would you like to meet first, the offensive or the defensive one?"

I have always regarded adversity as a challenge, as a great opportunity to learn and improve. When we face sufferings in the right spirit, we release the hidden potential in our spirit, from unconscious depths to the surface. I would go so far as to argue that adversity is essential for our spiritual progress.

To react to adversity with bitterness and anger defeats the Divine Plan. Rather, accept the challenge with gratitude, in the firm consciousness that "this too will pass away."

Christopher Reeves was the actor whom children adored as their own SUPERMAN. On film, he was the incredible wonder-man who performed terrific feats to help and save people. Everyone thought the world of him!

Reeves lost the use of his limbs in a tragic riding accident. Doctors almost lost hope of his survival in the dark days following his accident – but Reeves survived. He was confined to a wheelchair for the rest of his life – but he did not wallow in despair and misery. He devoted his life to raising funds for good causes and spreading the message of hope and cheer among the sick and the disabled. When he passed away, everyone grieved at the loss of a great-souled fighter!

What a wonderful way Reeves showed us to thank God in adversity!

"We brought nothing into His world," says the Bible. "And it is certain that we can carry nothing out." Therefore, all that comes to us during life is a gift from His holy hands.

Anna Quindlen was a successful writer and columnist. But she once confessed to a friend that she had attempted suicide more than once during her troubled, teenage years. How then, had she learnt to overcome her negative impulses and turn her life into a success?

Anna lost her mother to cancer, when she was young. The tragedy was a great learning experience for Anna. "I learnt that life was a great gift and I could not take it for granted," she writes.

We, too, need to realise that life is God's greatest gift to us. Each moment of this life is precious, and it needs to be cherished, treasured. Life needs to be lived fully – for its highs and lows, hopes and disasters, triumphs and failures – for they all have their own purpose and meaning.

"Inside yourself or outside, you don't have to change what you see, only the way you see it," says Thaddeus Golas.

The other day, I was agreeably surprised to see a friend who, not long ago, had been an invalid confined to bed. He was a heart patient, who also suffered from severe rheumatism. He had despaired of ever getting well again.

Imagine my astonishment when I saw him in fine fettle! He was the very picture of health and happiness. He had motored all the way from Secunderabad – a distance of several hundred kilometres. He had thoroughly enjoyed the trip and proposed to visit many places in North India before taking the return trip home.

In his illness, he told me, he had consulted many doctors, some of them eminent specialists. His condition, however, continued to deteriorate. He was a great believer in prayer, so he prayed to God for health and healing, but even that did not seem to help. His condition grew from bad to worse until his body was reduced to a bag of bones.

Then, one day, a feeling came over him to give up the wild chase that seemed to lead nowhere. He gave up consulting doctors. He stopped taking drugs. He ceased to pray for good health. He resolved that he would not ask God for anything except His Love. "Thy Love alone I seek, O Beloved of this broken, afflicted heart!" he cried again and again.

His prayer was soon answered. God revealed His Love to him, and, in a sudden flash, he saw that in all that happened to him was the loving hand of God. The pains from which he suffered, the bodily agony he had endured, day after day, all were according to the Divine Plan. It was the plan of Him who loved all humanity, all creation, with a love as boundless as the ocean.

The revelation filled him with such wondrous joy that rather than regaining good health and losing his newly found experience, he preferred to remain in his new state with a bedridden body. In a matter of days, however, he became well again, regaining his lost strength and health. Now this friend goes about from place to place, asking all who meet him, to seek God's love at all times. Did not Jesus say: "Seek ye first the Kingdom of God and all things shall be added unto Thee"?

People who have lost their loved ones all of a sudden, often learn to look at life from a new and more mature perspective. They become more sensitive to the little things of life. They are grateful for the rainbow in the sky, the laugh or cry of a child, the smile of a stranger. They realise that life is precious and offer gratitude to God – that their loved ones were allowed to be with them for so long.

We may not realise this – but all that we have, all that we are, have been given to us in God's goodness and wisdom. It is not that we have earned it or deserved it – He has loaned it to us. Adversity can help us in this awareness. When we thank God in adversity, we learn to stop the mad rush of existence; we *slow down* and allow ourselves to savour the great gift that is life.

It was the great essayist, Joseph Addison, who said, "Our real blessings often appear to us in the shape of pains, losses and disappointments."

True! The hardships, difficulties, trials and tribulations of life are all blessings – for they make us stronger and more self-reliant. It is right therefore, that we thank God for these. We curse the rain when it soaks our skin and ruins our clothes and shoes. But is it not the same rain that brings plenty to our fields and keeps our hunger at bay? It was a wise man who said that God brings men into deep waters – not to drown them, but to cleanse them.

Golda Meir was a remarkable lady who became the first woman Prime Minister of Israel. She was regarded as an astute politician, a tough leader, a great administrator. But she was not conventionally beautiful.

"Not being beautiful was a great blessing," she once remarked. "Not being beautiful forced me to develop my inner resources."

She knew the wisdom of Emerson's words: "For everything you have missed, you have gained something else."

A wife and mother of four children sighed as she faced the kitchen sink after dinner. It was overflowing with dirty dishes which she had to wash, dry and put away. Suddenly, she remembered the lines she had heard when she was a child:

Thank God for dirty dishes; they have a tale to tell:
While other folks go hungry we are eating pretty well.
With home and health and happiness, we shouldn't want to fuss;
For by this stack of evidence, God is very good to us!

No wonder William Shakespeare wrote: "Let me embrace thee, sour adversity, for wise men say it is the wisest course."

Let us thank God for sorrow – it teaches us pity and compassion. Let us thank God for pain and illness – we learn forbearance and patience. Let us thank God for friends who let us down and hurt us – for we learn the divine quality of forgiveness therefrom. Let us thank God for suffering – it teaches us courage. Let us thank God for disappointments – for they teach us to be ready for His appointment!

Charles de Gaulle, one of the most outstanding statesmen of the twentieth century, said: "A man of character finds a special attractiveness in difficulty, since it is only by coming to grips with difficulty that he can realise his potentialities." Is it not true that adversity is a springboard to great achievement?

A mother came to thank her Guru for the miraculous recovery of her child, who had been almost given up for lost.

"It was just as you said, Master," she said to him. "It was so good of God to give me back my child!"

"True," said the holy man. "But if your child had been taken away from you – would God have been still good and kind?"

The mother fell silent and did not reply.

It is so easy to give thanks and praise God's goodness and kindness when everything happens exactly as we want, and all our wishes are granted on demand. But if we are spiritually aware, we will thank God for *all* things at *all* times. For we should grow in the awareness that pleasure, gladness and gratification are *not* the most essential features of Thanksgiving.

A famous scholar, Matthew Henry, was once accosted by thieves, beaten and robbed of his purse. He wrote these words in his diary:

> Let me be thankful first, because I was never robbed before. Second, because although they beat me up, they spared my life. Third, because although they took all I carried with me, it was not much. And fourth, and most important of all, it was I who *was robbed*, not I who robbed.

110

When we thank God for the roses as well as the thorns, we have truly mastered the spirit of gratitude to God!

I read the real-life story of a woman who had escaped miraculously, when the two-seater plane in which she was travelling, crashed in a lonely, snow-covered hill slope. Her boss who was the pilot, was killed instantly. This woman suffered severe internal injuries and multiple fractures, but she survived the crash. Five hours later, she was rescued by a group of skiers and admitted to a rural hospital near by. After preliminary treatment, she was flown to a super speciality city hospital where she received the best treatment they could give her. Every doctor and nurse in the hospital had heard about the woman and her miraculous survival, for it had been on TV and all the newspapers – how she had panicked at first and lost all hope that she would ever be rescued alive; how the snow that blanketed her had actually protected her and kept her alive; and how the skiers had done their best for her. Everyone wanted to have a glimpse of the woman – for she would surely be a symbol of God's infinite mercy, and would have wonderful things to say in gratitude to the Lord.

But reality was otherwise. From the day she had been admitted to the hospital, she had nothing but complaints. "I'm fed up of being told that it is a miracle that I'm alive!" she cried. " You don't know what I have gone through! You don't know the agony and the pain I have suffered! Oh, fate has been cruel to me!"

She did not realise that the greatest miracle was that she was alive!

Helen Baker suffered from a nerve disorder which affected her neck, her body and her speech. She prayed constantly for healing and relief from pain – but she was never healed. At first she was angry, bitter and frustrated. But one day, she heard a voice within which said to her: "Helen, you will never ever be completely well – but you can use your infirmity to become a stronger woman and help other people."

Her whole attitude changed. Her severe physical handicap made her morally strong. She thanked the Lord for her condition and devoted herself to the welfare of others who suffered from the same rare form of illness. The most adverse condition did not stop her from expressing her thanks to the Lord!

No one can be truly happy, unless they are truly grateful for what they have – regardless of the circumstances.

When befriended, remember it. When you befriend, forget it.

— *Benjamin Franklin*

O thou who has given us so much, mercifully grant us one thing more – a grateful heart.

— *George Herbert*

One of life's gifts is that each of us, no matter how downtrodden, finds reasons for thankfulness.

— *J. Robert Meskin*

## Practical Suggestion No. 8
## Let Go, Let Go, Let God!

Life is full of problems, they tell me. True, but we must also remember that in God there is a solution to every problem.

Let go of your problems. Let God take over! Live like a child. Surrender yourself to the Lord in childlike trust and you will find miracles happening in your daily life.

Let go, let go, let God!

Are you frustrated, disappointed, hurt or unhappy? Do you find that even after you have put forth your best efforts, success seems to elude you? Then let me say this to you – Let go, let go, let God!

Let go of everything. Let God take charge of all your affairs! If only you can do this, you will find miracles happen in your daily life – and you will have a lot to be thankful for!

I suggest that you begin right away to repeat these magic words: Let go, let go, let God! As you continue to repeat this mystical formula, either silently or audibly, it will open the way for the flow of divine power into your life and you will be richly blessed!

A brother who is one of our Mission's devoted volunteers, fell seriously ill. The best of doctors could do nothing to help him recover. His wife was grief-stricken by his worsening condition. She wept, she shed bitter tears, she prayed to the Lord in despair. There seemed to be no answer. The man's condition became critical.

I suggested to the wife, "Let go, let go, let God!"

"What do you mean?" she asked.

"Let go of your husband," I said to her gently. "Do not cling to him. He does not belong to you. Surrender him to the Lord and let Him do what He will!"

The lady followed my advice and soon her husband began to recover. Today, I am happy to say, he is hale and hearty and always eager to help others.

Do you find yourself in a difficult situation? Are you passing through an emotional trauma? Are you in financial trouble? Are you filled with vague and nameless apprehension? Are you daunted by a difficult situation?

Then let go, let go, let God!

I assure you, you will not be disappointed. You will find your frustrations and fears dissolving. You will find that tension and unhappiness vanish like mist before the morning sun. You will find obstacles swept away, limitations washed out, and new opportunities opening before you. God will work through you to bring your highest good into visible expression in your life.

Letting go permits divine ideas to flow, divine light to shine, divine power to work, divine order and rightness to bless your life!

Letting go is an act of faith. And what is faith? Faith is not blind, as some people claim. Faith is *seeing* with the eyes of the heart. With our physical eyes, we behold the beauty of the world around us. But alas, in many of us the eyes of the heart are closed. When these eyes are opened, we will be able to see that all that has happened, has happened for the best, all that is happening, is happening for the best, and all that is yet to happen, will happen for the best.

There is a meaning of mercy in all that happens to us. For God has a plan for everyone of us, and there is a purpose in every incident, every accident that befalls us. The man of faith therefore, lets go... he moves on – ever onward, forward, Godward!

Faith is seeing with the eyes of the heart. The man of faith knows that when he lets go and lets God take over, everything will be taken care of in his life. For the Lord provides where He guides. And His ways are most mysterious.

Let go, let go, let God! Have faith that God is in charge of the Universe. He is the controller of the destiny of individuals and nations – and so nothing can ever go wrong!

To let go, is to seek refuge in the Lord. It is to trust Him – fully, completely, absolutely. It is to know that He is the one Light that ever shines. Though the storms howl and the darkness grows deeper, His light shines on! He is the Creator and Nourisher of all that is! He is the Deliverer from whom all evils flee. He is nearer to us than our heart-beats and closer than our breathing. He is the All-Powerful One whose presence is everywhere! Who needs anything else when He is our Friend and Helper? There is not a place too remote for His help to reach us. He is the All-Loving One whose ears are attentive to the prayers of His wayward children. He is the All-Knowing One who does the very best for us. With Him, all things are possible!

India is supposed to be a nation where people live by faith. But India has so much to learn from other nations. Indian currency bears images of our leaders. American currency carries the reassuring words: *In God We Trust*.

Did you know that the first U.S. coin to bear this inscription was a 2-cent piece minted in 1864? Salmon Chase was the Secretary of the Treasury under President Abraham Lincoln. He was a lover of God and man. In a letter to James Pollock, Director of the Mint, he wrote: "No nation can be strong except in the strength of God, or safe except in His defence. The trust of our people in God should be declared on our national coins." And so the inscription, *In God We Trust*, was born!

Blessed is the man who lets go and trusts God, turning to Him at every step. In God's loving, capable hands are the solutions to all our problems. In fact the happiest man is he who has allowed God to take over his life. Wherever he turns, he greets the love of God: he grows from more to more in the love of God.

Let go, let go, let God! He who lets God take over his life, knows that he is being led safely: and though he moves through fire and flood, the Lord is ever by him – what more can he need?

The man who lets go, is a man of true and deep prayer. He lifts up his heart to God at all times and seeks His help and guidance at every step. He has learnt to rely on God in all circumstances and so, when faced with danger or difficulty, he does not lose heart. His constant cry is, "On none but God do I rely. In Him do I trust. To Him do I turn!" Such a man has everything to be grateful for!

A much sought-after Christian preacher was asked to deliver a sermon at the local press club. They rang up to ask him the topic of the sermon.

"The Lord is my shepherd," he said.

"The Lord is my shepherd – is that all?" he was asked.

"That's enough," he replied.

The engagements column in the local paper carried the topic thus: "The Lord is my shepherd – that's enough."

The preacher was so delighted with this that he used the expanded version as his sermon title next Sunday!

Life has its share of disappointments, frustrations and failures. People let us down; events don't always follow our expectations; something is said or done that hurts us or vexes us. It is almost inevitable that we face such situations in life.

When we dwell persistently on such disappointments there are a few serious casualties we face – the loss of our joy, peace and inner contentment. How then, can we save ourselves from such negativism?

Let me tell you the story of a farmer, whose mule fell into a deep, disused well. For a minute or so, the farmer was stunned and grieved. The mule had indeed been a useful animal to him. Replacing it would be expensive; doing without it would be tough. But the well was too deep, and there was no way he could rescue it.

So the farmer decided that his faithful mule should be buried in the disused well. The mule was old, and the well was dry. He simply had to let go of both.

The farmer and his sons began to shovel mud into the well. As shovels full of mud fell on the mule's back, he stirred himself into action and shook off the mud, and clambered up. The more the mud was shovelled in, the harder he shook it off, and stepped up. In just a few hours, a weary and dirty mule stepped over the top of the well and on to safe ground!

We would do well to adopt the approach of the farmer: let go! And the attitude of the mule was not too bad either: shove off the dirt and clamber up!

God gave you a gift of 86,400 seconds today. Have you used one to say "thank you"?

*William A. Ward*

Stop complaining : start thanking.

*—J. P. Vaswani*

Dada J.P. Vaswani's inspirational books have reached out to thousands of readers worldwide, communicating, as only he can, his practical, down-to-earth approach to life and living, helping people to overcome problems and challenges and make the most of the great gift that is human life!

Dada's philosophy is not theoretical – it is the art of daily living; his spirituality is not abstract – it consists simply of thinking good thoughts, speaking good words and doing good deeds; his God is love, his religion is service and sacrifice. Dada is the very embodiment of humility and love.

Dada ennobles and illumines everything he touches. His books have proved to be bestsellers, and have been translated into several languages in India and across the world.

Admired and revered as one of the outstanding spiritual leaders of modern India, Dada has reached out to the hearts and spirits of people wherever he has travelled. Dada's exciting, new books in the *Life Guides* Series, have been compiled from the inspiring, uplifting talks that he has delivered to enthralled audiences all over the world.